T0193038

The Week's Problem
and other Canny Mathematics

BLEM SOLVING AND REAL LIFE MATHEMATICS PROBLEM SOLV-
AND REAL LIFE MATHEMATICS PROBLEM SOLVING AND REAL
MATHEMATICS PROBLEM SOLVING AND REAL LIFE MATHEMATICS
PROBLEM SOLVING AND REAL LIFE MATHEMATICS AND PROBLEM
VING AND REAL LIFE MATHEMATICS PROBLEM SOLVING AND REAL
MATHEMATICS PROBLEM SOLVING AND REAL LIFE MATHEMAT-
PROBLEM SOLVING AND REAL LIFE MATHEMATICS PROBLEM SOLV

Agnar Bergkuist
Translated from the Swedish
by **Malcolm Reid**

tarquin publications

If you enjoy this book, you might want to try its older sister book
Mathematical Snacks and *A Puzzle a Day* from Tarquin. You can buy Tarquin
titles from many bookshops and can see a list of major stockists on our website.
Alternatively, buy online at our or other major online retail
or request a catalogue to order direct from the address below

First published in Swedish
© Agnar Bergkuist 1996
Translation © Malcolm Reid 2011
ISBN 978 1 899618965
Printed in China

Tarquin Publications
Suite 74, 17 Holywell Hi
St Albans
AL1 1DT, UK
www.tarquingroup.com

Foreword

To the reader/problem solver

All real life mathematics is problem solving.

You can practise problem solving in different ways. In this book solving problems is approached differently from most mathematics books you have seen before:

• You get no clues to the type of calculation from the title

• Some problems may have no solution, whereas others may have many solutions

• Sometimes you can find a simple solution, but check very carefully to see if it is right. The problems are designed to be a little extra tricky.

The contents are divided into 4 categories with the answers at the back:

   *   problems
   **   problems (a little harder)
   ***   problems (can be quite tricky)
   The week's problem

The week's problems are intended to be solved in groups at school or maybe at home with the whole family. The other problems are often also best solved in a group. Part B contains harder problems than Part A: that is my intention at least. But what is easy for one solver can be almost impossible for another, and vice versa.

Neither of the parts need advanced mathematical knowledge, but despite this there are problems to which many adults either cannot find a straightforward solution or give the wrong answer (for Part B it is useful if you know what "percent" means).

Good luck!   **The Author**

Translator's Note

Born in 1931, Agnar was brought up on a small farm in Sweden with nine brothers and sisters. From a very young age he learnt practical work on the farm. Then he tried his hand at forestry and in a goldmine, before fulfilling his aspiration to train as a teacher with emphasis on music and maths.

He found himself working with textbooks of stereotyped parrot calculations and few exercises in problem solving. So he began developing his own problems from the pupils' world. Interest spread among colleagues and ultimately resulted in the publication of two booklets: *The Week's Problem*, Part A and Part B which sold well above expectations.

When I met Agnar in the 1996 his booklets seemed to fill exactly the sort of gap that I was experiencing in teaching the increasingly prescriptive UK mathematics curriculum and we agreed that I would translate and trial them here. Both booklets are combined into one volume of 120 problems.

I have used the problems in a variety of ways, including the school's monthly newsletter with a small prize for the first correct solution drawn out of a "post" box in assembly. To avoid any repetition, batches of problems were reserved for this and for particular year groups. You never run out of problems because after a while, pupils start coming with their own.

There isn't an age limit. Many of the problems can be solved either by a methodical slog, displaying perseverance, or by finding neat ways of looking at them, which is part of developing mathematical skills.

My most inspiring experience was with year 5 pupils (who were a SAT-free year group at the time), setting them a problem as an optional homework over each weekend. Family and friends could be involved, but the solution had to be written by the pupil. Marking was easy. I awarded one star for a correct basic solution and two stars for a well argued solution. It was a joy to see the variety of methods and the care taken over them, a step along the road to Agnar's goal of giving students the power to problem-solve in real life.

Malcolm Reid

The Week's Problem

Part A

One Star Problems

Number of Plants

*A1 Mr Smith wanted to grow a hedge with half a metre between plants. How long was the row if he had 40 seedlings?

Adding Problem

*A2 Replace the letters with figures so that the sum is correct.

Each letter always stands for the same figure.

```
    A  B  C
    A  B  C
+   A  B  C
   _____
    B  B  B
```

Lawn Race

*A3   Derek can mow his lawn in 1/3 hour.
Tom's lawn is 3 times as long and 3 times
as wide as Derek's, but Tom mows 3 times
as fast as Derek.

How long does Tom take to mow his lawn?
(Make a sketch if you wish.)

Box Total

*A4   A large box contains 5 smaller boxes. Each of these boxes
contains 5 little boxes which in turn contain 5 tiny boxes.

Annie takes out all the boxes and places them on her table.

How many boxes does she have?

Aching Hands

*A5 One day everyone in the class decided to shake hands with everyone else. There were 21 pupils altogether.

How many handshakes were there?

Odd Socks

*A6 20 pairs of socks are hanging in a dark attic. Half of them are black and half brown. The attic is so dark that you cannot see the difference between colours.

What is the smallest number of socks you need to take to be certain that:
(a) you get a pair?
(b) you get a brown pair?

Counting

*A7 Put in multiplication or addition signs in the right places between these figures so that the result is correct.

$$1 \quad 2 \quad 3 \quad 4 \quad 5 \quad 6 \quad 7 \quad 8 \quad 9 \;=\; 100$$

Note: you always do multiplication before adding.

Buster

*A8 When Suzie had paid her bus fare the driver said:

"Let's see. Three fifty plus two twenty, hmm, that makes six ten."

What did Suzie ask about?

Who Won?

*A9 5 girls took part in a race. Camilla didn't come first. Bridget came neither first nor last. Lizzie finished one place behind Camilla. Helen was not second. Mandy came 2 places behind Helen.

Write the finishing order.

Sort Times

*A10 It takes Alan 15 h (hours) to sort and fold 900 leaflets. Jenny does the same work in 10 h.

How long will it take if they do the job together?

Fish Catch

A11 Stephen and Mary sat fishing. After a while Stephen said:

"If you give me two fish, we will have the same number."

Mary replied: "If instead I get two from you, then I will have twice as many as you."

How many had each then caught?

Clock Chimes

A12 At 6 o'clock the church clock strikes 6 times. It takes 30 seconds from the first chime to the last.

How long will the clock take for 12 chimes?

The Sponge Cake

A13 How can you divide a sponge cake into 8 pieces with only 3 cuts?

The pieces do not need to be the same size.

Cubism

A14 A cube of side 3cm is painted green.
It is then sawn into centimetre cubes.

(a) What is the smallest number of cuts needed?

How many:
(b) small cubes are there
(c) have 4 green faces?
(d) have 3 green faces?
(e) have 2 green faces?
(f) have 1 green face?
(g) have no green faces at all?

Chain Reactions

A15 You have five short chains with 3 links in each (see picture). They have to be joined together in one long chain, by opening the smallest number of links.

How many links have to be opened?

Creepy Crawlies

A16 One day Karen came home from the woods with a jar of spiders and beetles. She said that there were 8 creatures in the jar with a total of 54 legs.

How many were spiders and how many were beetles?

Figure Play

*A17 Write the figures 9 8 7 6 5 4 3 2 1 in a row.

Write plus signs in the right places between the figures so that the sum is 99. (There are two solutions.)

Maths Book

*A18 Jonas looks through a book. In one place he multiplies the page numbers and gets the product 110. He turns back 2 pages and multiplies again.

What product does he then get?

Anderson's Fence

*A19 Anderson's plot is 35m wide and 40m long. How long will the fence round the plot be, if the garage drive is 4m wide and the path to the house is 2m wide?

Think About

*A20

A	A bicycle weighs	1Kg	5Kg	25Kg
B	How long is your bed?	50cm	100cm	200cm
C	A typical car weighs	500Kg	1 tonne	3 tonnes
D	1Kg coffee 1 Kg butter cost	the same	coffee is more	butter is more
E	The world's fastest runner goes at	36 kph	62 kph	87 kph
F	A TV licence costs (about) per year	£40	£90	£140
G	A year's pay of £20,000 is	low	average	high
H	One m³ air weighs	0g	10g	1Kg
I	The height of a ladder step is	11cm	17cm	26cm

Two Star Problems

Party

**A1 5 bakers decorate 5 cakes in 5 minutes.

How many cakes will 10 bakers decorate in 10 minutes?

Food Time

**A2 One day 8 people stood in front of you in the lunch queue. There was also exactly 2/3 of the queue behind you.

How many people were there in the queue?

Speed Question

**A3 On a motorway with a 110 kph speed limit a driver approached with a speed of 30 m/s.

Did he drive within the limit?

Cake Monster

**A4 Carl had two kinds of cake and 30 of each. The price was 10p for 2 of one kind, and 10p for 3 of the other kind.

Olga had the same number of cakes, but only one kind, which she sold at 20p for 5.

Both Carl and Olga sold all their cakes.

Who got most money?

Missing Cat

**A5 In a farmyard there were three cats: Fluff, Sooty and Tiddles. One day a cat came back with something in its mouth. If it had white paws it could be Fluff or Sooty. If it had no tail it was Sooty. If it had caught a mouse it could be Fluff or Tiddles. The cat which came back had caught a mouse, had black paws and a long tail.

What was it called?

Boat Trip

**A6 A father and his two sons wanted to cross a river in a little rowing boat. The father weighed 100 kg and the sons each 50kg. The boat could only carry 100kg.

How did they get over? (They couldn't swim.)

Weighty

**A7 A sack of potatoes weighs the same as 18kg + a quarter of a sack of potatoes.

How many kg does the sack of potatoes weigh?

Stools

**A8 You have 10 stools. These have to be placed along the walls of a square room so that there are 4 stools against every wall.

How can this be done?

Weightier?

**A9   Adam weighs 14kg more than Roger.
Together they weigh 114kg.

How much does each of them weigh?

Age-problem

**A10   When Jacob was 8 years old his father was 31.

Now Jacob's father is twice as old as Jacob.

How old is the youngster?

Exercise?

**A11 Peter set off into the woods one morning at 9 o'clock. Sometimes he ran, sometimes he walked and sometimes he rested. He rested 0·4 h, he ran 0·6 h, and he walked 3/5 h.

a) For how long did Peter run?

b) For how long did he walk?

c) When did he come home?

Kittens

**A12 Three cats, Pip, Sooty and Tiddles, had kittens.

Pip had twice as many as Sooty, while Tiddles had only a third as many as Pip.

How many kittens did each one have?

Register?

**A13 In class 5R there are 17 boys, of whom 9 were born in the first half of the year. Of the girls 4 were born in the first half of the year and twice as many in the second half.

a) How many pupils are there in the class?

b) How many were born in January?

Quick Grower

**A14 Brian went to visit his grandad. There he measured his height on a tree. His grandad made a mark in the bark.

Three years later, on another visit, he measured himself against the same tree and grandad made a new mark.

Brian had grown at 7cm a year and the tree at 18cm a year.

How big a gap was there between the old and the new marks?

Triangular

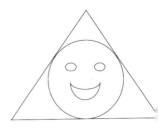

A15 The smallest possible triangle with all sides equal that you can draw round one circle looks like this:

With two circles on the base the triangle can contain a total of three circles:

a) How many circles can an equilateral triangle contain when there are 6 circles on the base?

b) Is there an equilateral triangle which can contain exactly 66 circles? If so, how many circles are there on the base?

Income

A16 For a summer job, Claire distributed leaflets for 2 hours a day every day of the week. Her hourly pay was £1.50. When she w ill for 3 days, Ann took over the job, but she wanted 50p an ho more. When Claire was well again, she also got the higher rate but now she could only work Monday to Friday.

Did Claire's weekly pay rise or fall? How big was the differen

Quadrilateral

A17 Try to draw a quadrilateral with three sides 3cm long and one side 6cm long.

Find out what such a figure is called if it has one line of symmetry.

Sunwarmth

A18 At her summer cottage 2-year old Julia used to bathe in a plastic paddling pool on the lawn. Her father had a long black hosepipe which lay in the sun. It was filled with water, and he emptied it into the pool. Julia wanted at least 18 l of water in the pool.
The hosepipe was 100m long.
The water in the hose was 26°C warm.
The hosepipe capacity was 2 dl/m and cost 65p per m.
The pool was red and could take 30 l.

Was the water in the hosepipe enough for Julia's bath?

What fraction of the pool was filled with water?

Perfect Squares

**A19 Malcolm's mathematics teacher, Bertie, was 17 when Malcolm was born.

At what ages will they simultaneously become perfect squares?

Note: A perfect square is the result when a number is multiplied by itself.

Pace

**A20 Robin and Emma decided on a car race. Robin drove the first half at an average speed of 100 m.p.h. but then the engine overheated and he drove the second half at 25 m.p.h.. Emma drove all the way at 50 m.p.h..

Who won and why?

Three Star Problems

Fake Coin

***A1** You have 9 similar coins, but one of them is a fake and lighter than the others.

What is the least number of weighings you must do with a beam balance to find the fake coin?

(You have no standard weights, so you can only compare weights.)

Numbers, Numbers...

***A2** The total 28 can be written with 5 twos and some plus signs like this:

$$22 + 2 + 2 + 2$$

Can you write the number 1000 in the same way with 8 eights and plus signs?

How does it Taste?

***A3** A can contains 10 litres of orange juice. Another can contains 10 litres of apple juice.

1 litre of orange juice is poured into the apple juice and the mix is shaken well.

Then 1 litre of the mixture is poured back.

Is there more orange juice in the apple juice than apple juice in the orange juice or are they perhaps the same?

Change

***A4** You have to pay £50 in notes.

In how many different ways can you do this?

Variant 1: without using £5 notes.

Variant 2: £5 notes may be used.

Tough Customs

***A5** A farmer bought a number of cows. To reach home he had to pass 4 customs posts. At each post they took half his herd but gave him back one cow. When he arrived home he had only 4 cows to put in the cowshed.

How many cows did he buy?

Floating Problem

***A6** A ship docks at a quay at low water. On the ship's side hangs a ropeladder with 32 steps. The distance between steps is 21cm including one step's thickness.

Each step measures 20cm × 10cm × 5cm. The ship's height above water is 7 metres. 52 minutes after docking it was high water. Between low and high water the water rose by 15 cm for every 72 seconds.

How many steps lay underwater after 42 minutes?

Uphill

***A7** The way up from the sea shore to the cliff-top is by three stairways with a space between each. The stairways have an average of 24 steps.

Jenny and John raced to see who would be fastest to the top. John took 2 steps at a time and 2 paces per second. Jenny took one step at a time and 3 paces per second. In each space Jenny gained 2 seconds.

Who won? By how much time?

A4-thoughts

***A8** A sheet of A4 is made by halving an A0 sheet 4 times. Each tin the long side is cut in the middle.

a) How many sheets of A4 are made from an A0?

b) Measure an A4 sheet (in mm). How big is an A0 sheet (rounded to the nearest cm)?

Not Fruitless

A9 When the ship Cecilia came into port, she was loaded with oranges from Jaffa. These were packed in 550 crates, each weighing 20 kg. A large crane with maximum load 2 tonnes loaded the oranges in half an hour.

(a) How many tonnes did the full load weigh?

(b) How many crates could the crane lift at a time?

(c) How many lifts were needed?

(d) How long did each lift take on average?

Football All Week

A10 32 teams took part in a football cup knock-out tournament. The team "We help one-another" won the cup.

a) How many matches did it play?

b) How many matches were played altogether in the tournament?

...and All Summer

***A11 "It's not fair", said the goalkeeper in the team "We are the best. We ought to play every team and the winner be the team with most points."

"Then we would have to play all summer," said one of the organisers.

(a) How many matches would each team have played given there are 32 teams?

(b) How many matches would be played in the whole tournament?

Familiar Look?

***A12 Solve the following cryptogram.

$$
\begin{array}{ccc}
  & A & C & B \\
+ & A & C & C \\
\hline
  & B & A & A \\
\end{array}
$$

Each letter always stands for the same number.

Knotty

***A13**   Oliver and Peter are friends.

Oliver's family have a sailing boat, while Peter's family spend their holidays at a farm.

Both of them practice sprinting and are good at 60 m (under 9 seconds).

One day Peter said:
"You talk only of sailing. I can certainly run faster than 5 knots."
" That's nothing", said Oliver. "I can run at 10 knots."
"Never", said Peter. "I bet you an ice cream."
"Then I win", said Oliver.

Could Oliver really run 60 m at a speed of 10 knots?

(Note: 1 knot = 1 sea mile/h, 1 sea mile = 1 852 m)

Week's Problem - Diffy

1. Draw as large a square as you can on your paper.

2. Choose any four numbers between 1 and 15 and place each at a corner of the square.

3. In the middle of each side write the difference between the two nearest corner numbers.

4. Draw a new smaller square with the new numbers at its corners.

5. Work out the differences again and write them in the middle of the sides.

6. Draw a new smaller square ....and so on.

What is the end result? Is it always the same? How many squares did you make? Who made the most? How many can you make?

This is an example of how it looks:

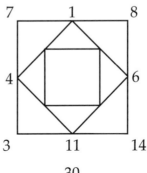

Week's Problem - Big T Puzzle

Copy or trace the figures below and build a big T

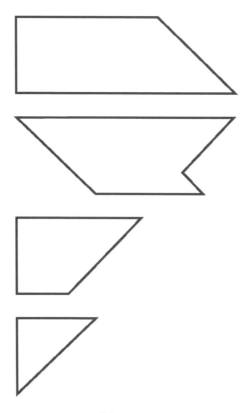

Week's Problem - Secrets

Anna, Bridget and Cecilia want to weigh themselves, but don't want anyone to know their weight. So they weighed themselves in pairs.

1. Anna and Bridget weighed 110 kg together.

2. Bridget and Cecilia weighed 110 kg together.

3. Anna and Cecilia weighed 120 kg together.

Afterwards Anna said:

"I can work out how much each one of us weighs."

Can you?

Week's Problem - Why?

Think of a number between 1 and 20.

Multiply it by 6 and add on 19.

Now subtract 7 and divide your answer by 6.

Take away the number you first thought of .

The answer is 2.

Try again with a new number.

Why is the answer still 2?

Week's Problem - Why?

Think of a number between 1 and 20.

Multiply it by 6 and add on 19.

Now subtract 7 and divide your answer by 6.

Take away the number you first thought of.

The answer is 2.

Try again with a new number.

Why is the answer still 2?

Week's Problem - Combination Puzzle

1. In a class there are 4 pupils.
2. Tom sits furthest to the left and loves soup.
3. Chris sits beside a pupil who likes meatballs.
4. Karen enjoys writing best and likes fish.
5. The pupil who prefers drawing loves mince.
6. The pupil who likes fish sits beside Tom.
7. The one who sits beside a white scarf likes meatballs best.
8. The blue scarf is on the left of the white.
9. Peter likes reading.
10. A girl wears the white scarf.
11. Chris has a yellow scarf.

Who has a red scarf?

Who likes counting?

Note: A table like the one below can be a useful help.

NAME				
SUBJECT				
COLOUR				
FOOD				

Week's Problem - Crossing Free

Try to draw each envelope below with one continuous straight line.

You may not go back over, cross or go along the same line more than once. Good luck.

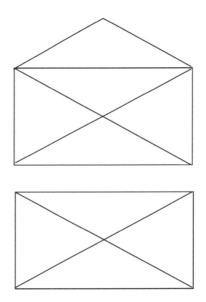

The Week's Problem

Part B

One Star Problems

Expensive Onion?

*B1 A hamburger with onion costs 60p.
The hamburger costs 50p more than
the onion.

How much is the onion?

The Portrait

*B2 Adolf and Josephine stood and looked at a portrait. Then
Josephine said:

"Who is that?"

"That man's father was my father's only son, was the reply."

Who was the portrait of?

No Bulldozer

*B3 Oliver and Peter want to dig a 50m long ditch. Oliver digs at 2 metres per hour and Peter at 3 metres per hour.

How long will it take them to dig the ditch?

Payments

*B4 For their ditch digging Oliver and Peter received £100 altogether.

How do you think they should share this fairly?

Strong Drinks

*B5 Karen and Lisa each mixed their own mugs of hot chocolate. Karen took 4 teaspoons of chocolate to 3dl milk and Lisa took 5 teaspoons to 4dl milk.

Whose drink was the stronger?

Old Problem

*B6 "How old are you, Grandpa?" asked ten year old Tina.

"Last year I was 22 times as old as you were, when you were a third as old as you are now, little Tina. How old do you think, that I am now?" asked Grandpa.

Snail's Pace

*B7 A snail wanted to climb up a 10m high flagpole. Each day it climbed 2m, but then slid down 1m each night. It started on Monday morning.

When did it reach the top?

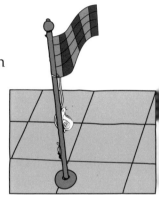

Eggy

*B8 Peter sells eggs. His first customer bought half of Peter's eggs + half an egg. The next customer bought half of what Peter had left + half an egg. Then Peter had 3 eggs left.

How many eggs did he have at the beginning?

A Question of Time

B9 Mr Flower expected to drive a stretch of 60 miles in one hour. Unfortunately by halfway he had only managed an average speed of 30 mph.

What speed must he keep for the other half in order to arrive in time?

Dotty

B10 Try, without backing or lifting the pencil, to join the 9 points with 4 connected straight lines.

• • •

• • •

• • •

Thick or Thin?

*B11 In numbering the pages of a book 201 figures are used. All the pages in the book are numbered.

How many pages does the book have?

More Figures

*B12 Using just one figure 5 times it is possible to make 100 in different ways. One example: 111 – 11 = 100.

Can you find 3 other ways?

You can use all the signs +, –, ×, ÷ and brackets if you want.

Heat Wave

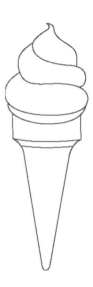

*B13 One day in May a year 5/6 class invited their teacher for an ice in an ice-cream bar.

Data:
There was one more pupil in year 6 than in year 5.
Each pupil in year 6 paid twice as much as each one in year 5.

The teacher's ice cost £1.30.

In year 5 they paid 5p per pupil.

How many pupils were from year 5?

How many from year 6?

How many pupils were in the class?

How many girls were there?

Ball-Boxes

*B14 A red, a green, a blue and a white ball are each put in a different box of the same colour as the ball.

a) How many ways are there of rearranging the balls so that only one is in a box of the wrong colour?

b) How many different ways are there of placing exactly two balls wrongly?

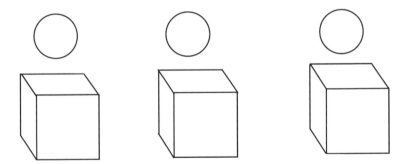

46

Two Star Problems

Animalish

**B1 In a barn there were the same number of cows, pigs and hens. Between them they had 60 legs.

How many animals were there altogether in the barn?

Book-Worm

**B2 Three books, I, II and III, stand in normal order from left to right on a bookshelf. A bookworm (which likes to eat books) has found itself between the cover and the first page of book I. It eats through and ends up between the cover and the last page of book III.
Each cover is 5mm thick and each book without the cover is 20mm thick.

How many millimetres did the bookworm eat through?
(Draw it!)

Big Win

**B3 Evan, Mark and Andrew were in a lottery syndicate. Evan paid in £2, Mark £3 and Andrew £4. They had a big win of £783 000.

How should the money be shared fairly?

Tied in Knots

**B4 The sum of a half and a quarter of a number is 18.

Work out the difference between a quarter and a half of the same number and multiply this difference by the number.

What is the result?

Goes Up in Smoke

**B5 Catherine's mother often complained about how expensive everything had got. Catherine suggested:

"Stop smoking and you will smell better and be healthier, more beautiful and so much richer that we could afford a holiday abroad for £700 every year."

Her mother smoked a packet of cigarettes (which cost £3.15 then) a day.

How much would Catherine's mother save in a month (30 days)?

Is Catherine really right about the holiday?

Checked

**B6 Mr Johnson's house had a window which was 1m high and 1m wide. He thought that it was too little and changed it for one with double the area, but the new window is also 1m high and 1m wide! Show with a drawing how the new and old windows could have looked.

49

Sporty?

**B7 One day in the winter sports holiday I skied on all the school's ski circuits, except the shortest. The circuits are 2·5km, 1·5km, 0·5km, 6km and 5km. Altogether I did 7 circuits, and no track more than twice. I skied a total of 25km.

Which tracks did I use?

Truth-Lies

**B8 Everyone in a room is either a liar or always tells the truth. A man in the room said:

"That girl in the corner told me that she is a liar."

Did the man tell the truth or did he lie? Explain.

Plant School

**B9 You are given the task of planting 16 fruit trees with exactly 10 straight lines containing 4 trees.

How can you do it?

Passing Time

**B10 The time is 9 am.

How many times will the minute hand have passed over the hour hand by 9 pm?

Stretching

**B11 A piece of elastic is 100 cm long. It can be stretched so that it is 25% (1/4) longer.

a) How long is the elastic then?

After that it pulls itself back so that it is 20% (1/5) shorter than when it was stretched.

b) How long is the elastic now?

Sale-Reduction

B12 The basketball team need to buy a new basketball for the summer matches. The sports shop had one for £24, but the same ball cost £26 in "NewSport". The sports shop offered the team a sale price with 25% off. Then "NewSport" said:

"We'll give you a £7·50 discount and also a one year's guarant worth £1."

Which do you think they should they buy from? Why?

Series Problem

B13   118, 199, 226, 235, 238, ?

What number should replace the question mark?

Parking Problem

B14 The parking sign outside the building where Emil's mother works says:

Mon–Fri 8–18 charges: 40p/hour
Month card: £45

Emil's mother says that she needs to park there 6 hours a day.

Does it pay for her to buy a month card? If so, how much would she save in a month with 23 working days?

New Times

B15 After a time Emil's mother's workdays were reduced to 15 days a month.

How does this change her parking calculations?

River Crossing

**B16 Matthew used to fish in the river with a rod. Once he cast too far so that the hook got stuck on the opposite bank. Matthew swam over to free it.

The river is 28 m wide. Matthew swims at a speed of 2m in 3 seconds. The water flow is 1/4 m/s. Matthew starts 10 m upstream and swims straight towards the opposite bank all the time.

How close to the hook does he land?

Upstream or downstream?

Something Missing

**B17 What numbers are missing in the following series?

(a)	1	2	4	7	?	16	?
(b)	3	7	15	?	63	127	?
(c)	2	4	?	256			

Tina's Number

**B18 Tina has written a 2-digit number in her book. The product of the digits in her number is 16.

(a) What numbers can you find which fit?

(b) If Tina's number is divisible by 11, which is her number?

(c) If Tina's number minus 2 is divisible by 10, which is her number then?

Tina's other Number

**B19 Tina wrote a new number in her book. The number had either two or three digits. The product of the digits in this number is 16.

(a) What numbers can you find that fit?

(b) If Tina's number minus 12 is divisible by 100 (ends with 00), what is her number?

(c) If Tina's number plus 7 is divisible by 9 and 5, what is her number?

Three Star Problems

Fake Coins

***B1** You have 10 piles with 15 coins in every pile. One of the piles contains fake coins, which are 0·5g heavier than the real coins which weigh 10 grams each. You have a very exact scale which shows weights with an accuracy of 0·1g.

How can you with one single weighing decide which pile contains the fake coins?

Difficult Carpentry Problem

***B2** A saw, a knife and a rule together cost £14.

The saw costs £9 more than the knife.

The saw and knife together cost £12 more than the rule.

What is the cost of each tool?

Swim Time

***B3 My neighbour has a pool that can be filled in 10 hours. When he empties it, it takes 15 hours. Once he had forgotten to put in the plug before filling the pool.

How long did it take to fill then?

Profit or Loss

***B4 A man sold two golf clubs for £120 each. On one he made a 20% profit, on the other he made a 20% loss.

How much did he lose or gain overall on the deal?

Post Problem

***B5** A 6m long rope hangs between 2 posts. One post is 4m high and the other is 3m high. A weight hangs in the rope and keeps it taut. The weight hangs half a meter above ground.

What is the distance between the poles?

On Macdonald's Farm

Beware the Hidden Legs

***B6** Old MacDonald had a farm, as we all know.

In the stables were horses and flies, which altogether had 51 heads and 300 legs.

How many horses did Old MacDonald have?

Peter and Paul

B7 One day I met Peter and Paul who have similar looks. When I asked if they were related, Peter said:

" I have neither sisters nor brothers, and this man's father is my father's only son."

Can you work out how they are related?

Paleface's Death

B8 The Indian chief Pale Death is going by train for the first time in his life. He is as usual armed with his bow and arrow. He stands on the back of the last carriage so that he can shoot backwards. He knows that his arch enemy general White Face is standing beside the track. The Indian prepares himself to shoot when the train passes. The speed of the train is 180 km/h. At the right moment Pale Death shoots his arrow, which has the speed of 50 m/s.

Can the arrow reach its target, assuming the Indian has aimed correctly?

Avenue Improvement

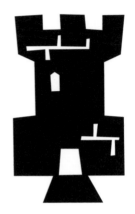

***B9** A long old avenue of trees led up to Drumwick Castle.

Over time a number of trees had died and needed replacement. Each sapling cost £4.

On one side every 5th tree had died, and this came to 12 trees. On the other side a quarter of the trees had died.

a) How many trees were there originally?

b) How many new saplings needed to be bought?

c) How much did this cost if you wanted to have 3 spare saplings?

Dog's Work

***B10 Victoria was going to be 10. Most of all for her birthday she would like a dog, a sweet little puppy which she could look after all by herself. Her parents were very hesitant.

"Can you get up half an hour earlier each morning to take the dog out?" Daddy asked and Victoria said yes. "Have you thought about the cost?" Mummy said. "Maybe we should do some calculations."

A tin of dog food costs £1·50 and lasts a week. Coat trimming and nail clipping twice a year cost £40 each time. Deworming and visits to the vet cost about £30 a year. Victoria had £3 a week for pocket money. In addition she looked after her little brother some evenings and got £4 a month for that. Victoria thought for a while and then said:

"I can manage that and still have some money over."

Did she work it out correctly?

If so, about how much did she have left each week?

Bussing

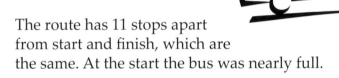

***B11   A town bus on a circular route has 65 seats.

The route has 11 stops apart from start and finish, which are the same. At the start the bus was nearly full.

At the first five stops no new passengers got on, but at each stop half the passengers plus half a person got off. At stop number six the rest got off, which was one person. At the same time some people got on.

At stops 7, 8, 9, 10 and 11 the number of passengers was doubled each time and when the bus got back to the terminal there was only one free seat.

How many passengers were on the bus at the start?

How many got on at stop number 6?

Throw Of A Die

***B12** "I have two dice, a white and a black, which each have a side which comes up almost all the time," said Lindsay. "Which sides?" asked Clara.

"I won't say. You will have to find out yourself," was the reply.

Clara threw the white die 10 times. She got the same number 8 times. The sum of all the throws was 49.

When she threw the black die 10 times again Clara got the same number 8 times, but this time the sum was 21.

What was the number that came nearly all the time on the white die?

And on the black?

Which numbers came up on the two other throws with the white die? Which two on the black?

Shape Thoughts

***B13 (a) How many sides do each of the above shapes have?

(b) How many edges?

(c) Draw, cut out and glue together a shape with 4 identical faces. What is this shape called?

(d) Can you make a shape with 5 faces (which don't need to be the same shape)?

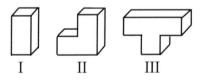

I   II   III

Ball Boxes

***B14 The tennis club's U 14 team was going on a training weekend. 45 tennis balls were in a big wooden box in the club house. Harry was going to make sure that they took all the balls.

He measured a ball and found that the diameter was 6 cm. He then went to the shop to find a suitable container. There were boxes in 3 different sizes with the following measurements in cm:

	Length	Breadth	Height
A	36	18	13
B	30	18	18
C	30	24	13

Which box should he choose to fit in all the tennis balls?

The Smith Family

***B15** The Smith family consists of Mum, Dad, Angela, Tony and little brother Oliver. Mum is 3 years older than Dad and together the parents are 81 years old. Angela is 2 years older than Tony, who is 5 years older than Oliver. Together the children's ages come to 21.

How old is each member of the Smith family?

Grandfather Clock

***B16** Uncle's big grandfather clock chimes every hour with as many "dongs" as the hour. It also chimes with a "ding" at quarter past the hour, 2 "dings" at half past the hour and 3 "dings" at a quarter to the hour. Of course the clock chimes only once at 13.00 etc.

(a) How many "dongs" has the clock chimed between 9.25 and 15.10?

(b) How many "dings" has the clock chimed during the same time?

Fishing Luck

***B17** In the river where Roger used to fish, you could catch
many different kinds of fish. A group of youngsters had
worked out the following points system:

  perch 5, pike 10, trout 15, whitefish 20, salmon 40.

One day their catch was as follows:

	Number of fish	Number of points
Bert	2	15
Eleanor	7	50
Karen	8	100
Larry	4	125
Roger	8	45
Sarah	11	65
William	5	40

What fish and how many of each kind had each of them
caught?

Are there other alternatives?

Oldies

***B18** Peter is one year younger than his sister Lisa, and they also have a little brother. They all go to school. One day Peter frowns and says:

"Think. If you add the squares of little brother's age and my age together, you get exactly the same as the square of Lisa's age. Weird Eh?"

How old are the children?

Note: You get a square by multiplying a number by itself.

Dogs

***B19** A bowl of dog biscuits for the family's dogs, a bitch and three puppies, stood in a corner. The bitch came first and ate up half the biscuits and one more biscuit. Then the biggest puppy came and did the same. The second and the third puppy followed suit. When the neighbour's dog arrived the bowl was empty.

How many biscuits were in the bowl from the start?

Week's Problem - Combination Problem

In a street there are 5 houses painted different colours. In each house lives a single man. Each man comes from a different country and drinks only one kind of drink.

1. The Swede drinks coffee.
2. In the blue house the man drinks squash.
3. The Chinese drives a Mazda.
4. The blue house is to the right of the yellow one.
5. The man who drinks tea drives a Volvo.
6. The Russian lives in the middle.
7. The man who drives a SAAB lives next to the yellow house.
8. The Chinese lives to the right of the Russian.
9. The Finn lives to the left of the coffee drinker.
10. The red house is next to the yellow one.
11. The man in the green house drinks milk.
12. In the white house the man drives a Toyota.
13. The American lives next door to the Chinese.

Who drinks juice? Who drives a Ford?

House colour					
Country					
Drink					
Car make					

Note:
This kind of table can be helpful.

Week's Problem - Large Grids

How many different 2-D shapes can you make from

a) 2 identical squares?

b) 3 identical squares?

c) 4 identical squares?

d) 5 identical squares?

Note: Each square should have at least one side in common with another square. A shape doesn't count as different if it is a reflection or rotation of an existing shape.

Week's Problem - Bouncing Numbers

Choose a number between 10 and 20.

Keep dividing by 2 until the result is an odd number.

Then multiply by 3 and add 1.

Keep dividing by 2 again until the result is an odd number.

Multiply again by 3 and add 1.

Continue in this way until you see a pattern. What is it?

Try another number. Do you get the same pattern?

Which is the highest number you reach before it starts going down?

How many multiplications do you need to do before you get to the bottom?

Which number under 20 reaches the highest value?

Week's Problem - House Construction

Some years ago the Elliott family planned to build a house.

The foundations were 14m long and 8.5m wide for the house and 6m x 5m for the garage. The foundations needed to be filled with sand to an average depth of 40cm.

The truck which transported the sand had a capacity of $8m^3$.

The sand weighed 1800 kg/m^3.

The truck used ¼ diesel fuel per mile. Diesel cost 99p per litre.

The distance from the truck base to the building site was 18 miles.

The sand store was 21 miles from the building site.

Sand cost £12/m^3.

The truck driver wanted £23 per load and £20 for driving to and from the site, on top of the fuel bill.

(a) How many cubic metres of sand were needed (to the nearest m^3)? How many truck loads was this?

(b) How many tonnes of sand was this altogether?

(c) How much was the fuel bill for the truck?

(d) How much was the Elliott's bill for both sand and its transport?

Week's Problem - Always the Same?

1. Choose a four figure number where not all the digits are the same.

2. Put the digits in order from the largest to the smallest.

3. Now make a number with the same digits in reverse order.

4. Find the difference.

Repeat steps 2–4 with your answer and keep going. What happens?

Is it the same with a different starting numbers?

Week's Problem - Lost Deal?

A man came into a cycle shop to buy a bicycle. He chose one which cost £170 and paid with a traveller's cheque for £200. The shopkeeper went over the road to the bank, cashed the cheque and gave the customer £30 change. The customer then cycled away.

Soon afterwards the bank clerk came over and said that the cheque was forged. He wanted his £200 back.

The shopkeeper then went to a good friend and borrowed £200 which he gave to the bank.

The lost bike had cost the shopkeeper £125 wholesale. Now the question is: how much did he lose in this deal?

Week's Problem - The Party

Larry and Karen were going to have a party.

Larry bought 6 bottles of squash. On the bottles it said:
Contents 7 dl. Mix: 1 part squash to 4 parts water.

Karen and Larry reckoned that they and their party guests would drink 3 glasses of squash each. Then the squash would be exactly the right amount.

The squash cost £1.64 a bottle.

The biscuits were packed in boxes of 10. The boxes were £1.29 each.

Larry had £1.50 a week for pocket money whilst Karen, who was older, had £2 a week.

(a) For how many glasses (2 dl) of mixed squash had he planned?

(b) How many guests were Karen and Larry planning to invite?

(c) How many biscuits should Karen buy if they thought that everyone would have 4 biscuits each?

(d) How much did Karen and Larry pay together if their guests each paid 50p?

(e) How much should each of them pay?

Week's Problem - Triangular Affair

How many triangles are there in this picture?

Count all of them, big and small, the right way up and upside down.

Clue: There are 5 different sizes.

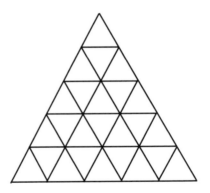

The Week's Problem

Answers

A* Answers

*A1   19.5 m

*A2   A = 1, B = 4, C = 8

*A3   1 hour

*A4   156 boxes

*A5   210 (20 + 19 + 18 + …)

*A6   (a) 3 socks (b) 22

*A7   One way: 1 + 2 + 3 + 4 + 5 + 6 + 7 + 8 × 9 = 100

*A8   Journey time

*A9   Helen, Bridget, Mandy, Camilla, Lizzie

*A10   6 hr (work out 1st the number of leaflets per hour)

*A11   Stephen 10, Mary 14

*A12   66 secs. Count the gaps

*A13   Include one horizontal cut ⟶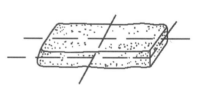

*A14   (a) 6 (b) 27 (c) 0 (d) 8 (e) 12 (f) 6 (g) 1

*A15   3, all in the same chain

*A16   5 beetles, 3 spiders (spiders have 8 legs, beetles 6)

*A17   One way: 9 + 8 + 7 + 65 + 4 + 3 + 2 + 1

*A18   The product is 42

*A19   144 m

*A20   Group discussion

A** Answers

**A1 20 (1 baker decorates 1 tart in 5 mins)

**A2 27 pupils (8 + you = 1/3)

**A3 Yes. His speed was 108 kph.

**A4 Carl, 10 p more than Olga.

**A5 Tiddles

**A6 1st both sons rowed over and one back. Then the father rowed over alone, after which the other son fetched his brother.

**A7 24 kg (3/4 of a sack is 18 kg)

**A8 One way: 2 on top of each other in 2 diagonal corners, one in each of the other 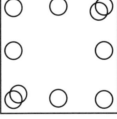 corners and one on each side.

**A9 Adam 64 kg, Roger 50 kg.

A10 23

A11 (a) 36 min (b) 36 min (c) 10.36 a.m.

A12 Sooty had 3, Pip 6, Tiddles 2 (6, 12, 4 unlikely)

A13 (a) 29 pupils (b) Insufficient information to answer

A14 21 cm (trees grow only from the top)

A15 (a) 21 circles (b) yes. 11 circles on the base.

A16 It fell by £1 per week.

A17 First part, many solutions. With symmetry, trapezium as shown.

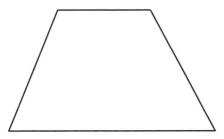

A18 Yes. The pipe contained 20 litres and 2/3 filled the pool.

A19 64 and 81.

A20 Emma. Test the times taken for say a 100 mile course.

A*** Answers

***A1 2 weighings. 1st put 3 coins on each pan.

***A2 888 + 88 + 8 + 8 + 8 = 1000

***A3 Equally much

***A4 Without £5 notes: 4 With £5 notes: 13

***A5 34 cows (begin at the end)

***A6 The ship floats!

***A7 John by 2 secs

***A8 (a) 16 sheets of A4 (b) about 84 cm × 119 cm

***A9 (a) 11 tonnes (b) 100 crates (c) 6 lifts (d) 5 min

***A10 (a) 5 matches (b) 31

***A11 (a) 31 (b) 496 matches!

***A12 A = 3, B = 7, C = 6

***A13 Yes. 10 knots is 60 m in 11.66 secs.

A: *The Week's Problem. Answers*

Diffy: The end result is always 0.

Big T Puzzle: There is a solution

Secrets: Anna 60 kg, Bridget 50 kg, Cecilia 60 kg (from 1 & 2 Anna & Cecilia weigh the same)

Why? Try with 0. You multiply by 6, add 12 and divide by 6 giving 2. Any other start number is taken away at the end.

How Does it Work? × 2, + 3, × 5, –11 is equivalent to × 10, + 15 – 11 or × 10 – 4. Cross out the 4 and you get your starting number

Combination Puzzle: Peter has a red scarf. Tom likes counting.

Crossing Free:

Here is one solution
for the envelope
with the open flap

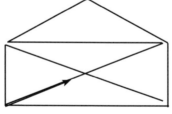

START   FINISH

2nd one is impossible as there are 4 odd 'nodes'. You can only start or finish at an odd node.

B* Answers

*B1   5 p

*B2   Adolf's son

*B3   10 hr

*B4   Either equally, or Oliver £40 and Peter £60

*B5   Karen's (4/3 › 5/4)

*B6   67 (66 last year)

*B7   Tuesday the following week

*B8   15 (work backwards)

*B9   He has already used up his hour so he can't do it

*B10

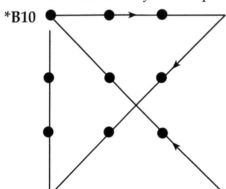

*B11   103 pages

*B12 $5 \times 5 \times 5 - 5 \times 5$

$(5 + 5 + 5 + 5) \times 5$

$3 \times 33 + 3/3$

*B13   8 in year 5, 9 in year 6, 17 altogether, no. of girls unknown

*B14   (a) no

(b) 6

Box colour:

The ones in the shaded area are in the correct box

Red	Green	Blue	White
R	G	W	B
R	W	B	G
R	B	G	W
W	G	B	R
B	G	R	W
G	R	B	W

B** Answers

**B1   18

**B2   40 mm (Stand the books on a shelf and see where the 1st and last pages are.)

**B3   Evan £1 74 000, Mark £2 41 000, Andrew £3 48 000
(Divide the winnings by the sum of their stakes. Then multiply th
by each of their stakes in turn.)

**B4   144 (1/2 + 1/4 = 3/4, so the number is 24)

**B5   £94.50. Yes. She would save about £1150 a year.

**B6   One solution: The window has 1st the shape of a triangle with a b
of 1 m and a height of 1 m, and is then changed to a square. There
are other solutions.

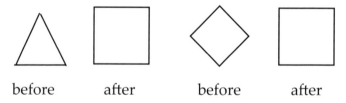

before   after   before   after

**B7   One solution: 2 × 1.5, 2 × 2.5, 2 × 6, 1 × 5

86

**B8 He lied. In these conditions everyone must say that they are telling the truth.

**B9

```
*       *       *       *
*       *       *       *        Lines not
*       *       *       *        necessarily at
*       *       *       *        right angles.
```

**B10 11 times.

**B11 (a) 125 cm (b) 100 cm

**B12 Prices: Sports shop £18, "New Sport" £18.50. The guarantee's worth can be discussed.

**B13 239 (differences: 81, 27, 9, 3, 1)

**B14 Yes. She gains £10.20 a month.

**B15 It is £9 cheaper per month to pay daily.

**B16 Half a metre downstream.

**B17 (a) 11, 22 (Add on 1, 2, 3, 4 etc.)
(b) 31, 255 (x 2 + 1)
(c) 16 (square)

**B18 (a) 28, 44, 82 (b) 44 (c)82

**B19 (a) 28, 44, 82, 128, 144, 182, 218, 224, 242, 281,414, 422, 441, 812, 821
(b) 812
(c) 128 or 218

B*** *Answers*

***B1** Take one coin from the 1st pile, 2 from the 2nd, 3 from the 3rd etc. The scale shows how many grams too heavy the collection is.

***B2** The rule costs £1, the knife £2 and the saw £11.

***B3** 30 hr (Suppose that the pool contains for example 30 000 l).

***B4** He lost £10 (gain = £20, loss = £30).

***B5** The posts are right next to each other.

***B6** 3 horses (and 48 flies).

***B7** Peter was Paul's father.

***B8** The train's speed, 180 kph = 50 m/s. This results in the arrow dropping straight down if it is shot backwards, without any chance of hitting anything other than the ground.

***B9** (a) 120 trees (b) 27 (c) £120.

***B10** Yes. She gets about 30p on average a week left over.

***B11** 63 at the start. 2 got on at stop 6.

***B12** Secret number: 5 on the white and 2 on the black die. Other scores: 6 and 3 on the white; 1 and 4 on the black.

***B13 (a) I 6, II 8, III 10
(b) I 12, II 17 + 1 inside, III 22 + 2 inside.
(c) a tetrahedron.
(d) e.g.: a pyramid with a square base.

***B14 B (fits 5 × 3 × 3 balls)

***B15 Mum is 42, Dad 39, Angela 10, Tony 8 and Oliver 3

***B16 (a) 39 dongs (b) 35 dings

***B17

	Perch	Pike	Trout	Whitefish	Salmon
Bert	1	1			
Eleanor	6			1	
Karen	4			4	
Larry	1				3
Roger	7	1			
Sarah	10		1		
William	3	1	1		

There are other alternatives.

***B18 The little brother is 5, Peter 12 and Lisa 13

***B19 30 (work backwards)

B The Week's Problem Answers

Combination Problem

The Chinese drinks juice. The Finn drives a Ford. (Fill in the certainties
1st: 6, 8, 13, 3, 1, 9. Then put the blue house somewhere and see if
it works.)

Large Grids

Look out for rotations and reflections. If you work on squared paper
and cut out the shapes, you can see more easily which figures rotate
or reflect (turn over) onto one another.
(a) 1 (b) 2 (c) 5 see below (d) 12

Bouncing numbers

An end loop: 4 > 2 > 1 > 4…160

Up to 20 (Which starter would give you 20?)

15

House Construction

(a) 60 m³, 8 loads (b) about 110 (107–108 tonnes).
(c) If we assume that the truck driver began the day by driving to the building site (and not directly to the sand store) 372 miles and £92.07. Such accuracy is meaningless since the fuel consumption varies greatly, especially between loaded and unloaded. A suitable rounding could be £90.
(d) Driver's cost £204. Sand cost £720. So total around £1020.

Always the same?

Sometimes you get 0. Other times you get repetitions of 7641. Are there any others? (You should insert 0s on the left to keep to 4 digits each time.)

Lost Deal

£155 (Cycle's £125 + £30)

The Party

(a) 105 glasses of squash
(b) 33 guests
(c) 140 biscuits (incl. Larry and Karen)
(d) £11.40 e) Equal shares or…?
Can be discussed.

Triangle Drama

48 (25 small 1-ers; 13 4-ers; 6 9-ers; 3 16-ers; 1 25-er)

Other Books from Tarquin

Tarquin produces a number of books that will be of interest to anyone who has enjoyed using this book. You can see all our titles on www.tarquingroup.com or contact us using the details below for a catalogue. Have a look at the following books especially, as all of them contain mathematical and logic puzzles suitable for use in school or for fun

Mathematical Snacks

A Puzzle a Day

Who Tells the Truth

The Number Puzzler

Tarquin Number Challenges

The Number Detective

Tarquin
Suite 74, 17 Holywell Hill
St Albans AL 1 1DT
United Kingdom
info@tarquingroup.com